EDGE BOOKS

# THE SCIENCE BEHIND ATHLETICS

by Lisa J. Amstutz

London 2012

HARDEE

USA

raintree

a Capstone company — publishers for children

Raintree is an imprint of Capstone Global Library Limited, a company incorporated in England and Wales having its registered office at 264 Banbury Road, Oxford, OX2 7DY – Registered company number: 6695582

www.raintree.co.uk
myorders@raintree.co.uk

Text © Capstone Global Library Limited 2016
The moral rights of the proprietor have been asserted.

ISBN 978 1 4747 1141 8
19  18  17  16  15
10 9 8 7 6 5 4 3 2 1

**British Library Cataloguing in Publication Data**
A full catalogue record for this book is available from the British Library.

**Editorial Credits**
Arnold Ringstad, editor
Craig Hinton, designer and production specialist

**Photo Credits**
AP Images: 21 (top), David Davies/Press Association, 16, David J. Phillip, 1, 6–7, 29, Hassan Ammar, 22, Kyodo, 27, Lefteris Pitarakis, 12–13, Mark Baker, 14–15, Matt Dunham, cover, 4, 19, 24, Mike Groll, 8, Pawel Kopczynski, 26; Dorling Kindersley, 23; Dorling Kindersley/Thinkstock, 4–5, 18–19, 21 (bottom); Red Line Editorial, 10–11, 28; pictorico/iStockphoto, 11

We would like to thank Mark Walsh, Associate Professor of Exercise Science at Miami University, Oxford, Ohio, for his help in the preparation of this book.

Printed in the United States of America in North Mankato, Minnesota
102015    2015CAP

# CONTENTS

Jamaica's Usain Bolt dashes towards victory in the 100-metre sprint at the 2012 London Olympics.

**long jump/ triple jump**

/////////

**ATHLETICS**
ARENA ○○○○○

**hammer throw**

**discus**

# CHAPTER 1

# GOING FOR GOLD

**H**eads down and feet on the starting blocks, the runners wait. Bang! The starting pistol fires, and they're off. Arms and legs pumping, they race for the finish line with a single goal in mind: an Olympic medal. Who will be the next champion?

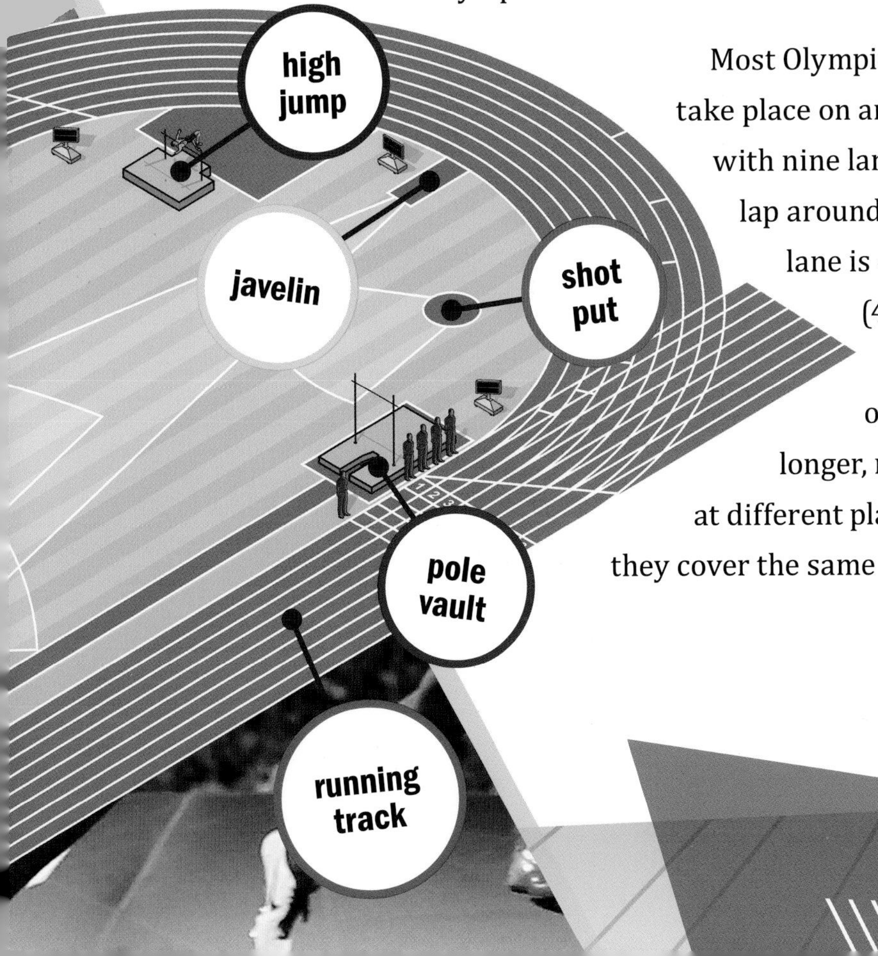

Most Olympic races take place on an oval track with nine lanes. One lap around the inside lane is 400 metres (437 yards). Since the outer lanes are longer, runners start at different places. That way they cover the same distance.

**high jump**

**javelin**

**shot put**

**pole vault**

**running track**

# FIGHTING FORCES

**drag**

In the javelin throw, the force of an athlete's throw is working against two naturally occurring forces. The first is drag, or air resistance. As the javelin flies, it collides with air molecules. The collective force of these collisions slows down the javelin. The second force is gravity. Gravity attracts objects with mass towards each other. Since Earth is so much larger than the javelin, this force is only noticed in one direction. The javelin is pulled towards the centre of the planet.

**gravity**

throwing
force

Jumping and throwing events are held on a large field inside the track. The field is covered with grass or artificial turf. Long jumpers land in a sandpit. High jumpers and pole-vaulters land in mats filled with soft padding, known as pits.

## The science of athletics

Great athletes make their sports look easy. But nothing could be further from the truth. They train hard and make every motion count. They use their knowledge of physics to their advantage, working with **drag**, **gravity** and **momentum**. Understanding the science of the sport can shave seconds off a racer's time. It can give a discus thrower the extra millimetre needed to win.

**drag** force that slows an object in motion travelling in air or water
**gravity** force that causes objects to move towards Earth's centre
**momentum** mass of an object multiplied by its speed

Uganda's Stephen Kiprotich won the gold medal in the 42.2-kilometre (26.2-mile) men's marathon race at the 2012 London Olympics.

# CHAPTER 2

# RUN LIKE
# THE WIND

The world's fastest runners compete at the Summer Olympics every four years. They walk or run races ranging from 100 metres (109 yards) to 50 kilometres (31 miles).

Drag is the force that slows these athletes the most. Air may look like empty space, but it is filled with countless molecules of invisible gas. The result of running into these molecules is drag. Sprinters wear tight clothing to reduce the amount of surface area struck by the air as they move. This lets them move faster.

## What about wind?

Have you ever tried to run on a windy day? The wind can push you along or slow you down. Wind affects Olympic runners in the same way. It can increase or decrease the amount of drag. A runner's time does not count as a world record if a wind stronger than 2 metres (6.6 feet) per second is blowing at her back. Too much wind gives a runner an unfair advantage.

## On the fast track

At the 2012 London Olympics, Usain Bolt defended his gold medal in the 100-metre sprint. He ran the distance in 9.63 seconds, an Olympic record. The biomechanics of Bolt's sprinting give him an edge over his competitors. At 1.96 metres (6 feet, 5 inches), he stands taller than the typical sprinter, giving him a long stride length. Most sprinters take 44 steps to complete the 100-metre race, but Bolt needs only 41.

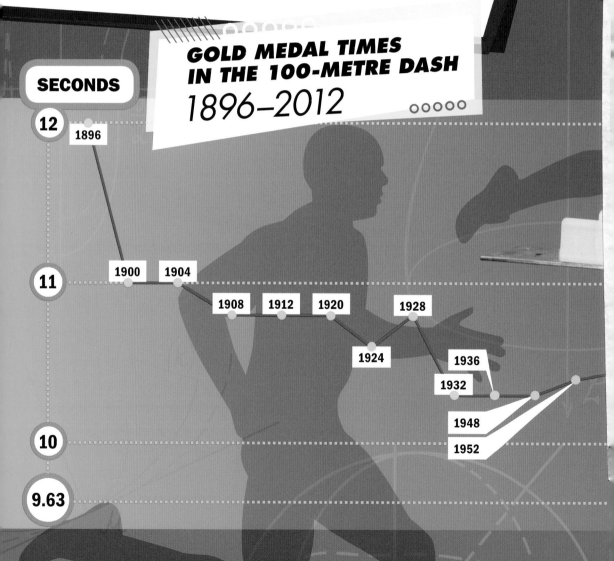

## GOLD MEDAL TIMES IN THE 100-METRE DASH
### 1896–2012

**SECONDS**

12 — 1896

11 — 1900  1904

1908  1912  1920  1928

1924

1936
1932

1948

10 — 1952

9.63

Sprinters need a burst of power to speed up quickly. They place their feet against starting blocks and push off. Sir Isaac Newton's third law of motion says that for every action there is an equal and opposite reaction. The block does not move when a sprinter pushes on it. So the force from the sprinter's foot pushes against his body instead. This propels him forward at the start of the race and helps him reach his top speed as soon as possible.

The action of a sprinter's push against the starting block causes a reaction that accelerates the runner forwards.

1956

1960

1964

1980

1972

1968

1976

1984

1988

1992

1996

2000

2004

2008

2012

**9.63**
Olympic record

In race walking, competitors must have one foot touching the ground at all times.

## Going the distance

Can you imagine running 42.2 kilometres (26.2 miles) without stopping? That's exactly what marathon runners do. The marathon is the longest Olympic running event. Race walkers cover even more ground in the 50-kilometre race.

Distance runners use energy in a different way to sprinters. They do not move as fast, but they must go much further. They train for **endurance** as well as speed.

Even the muscles of sprinters and distance runners differ. Fast-twitch muscle fibres move fast. They also get tired fast. Slow-twitch fibres react more slowly. But they can keep going much longer. Sprinters have more fast-twitch fibres in their muscles. Marathon runners have more slow-twitch fibres.

Distance runners try to save energy when they can. One way is by **drafting**. The first runner pushes air out of the way. The second runner has less air to push against. He conserves energy because there is less drag to fight.

**endurance** ability to remain active for a long time
**draft** to run close behind another runner to lessen air resistance

## Winning the race

The end of the race is near, and the finish line in sight. The sprinters flash by in a blur. The race is too close to call. Luckily, high-tech finish-line cameras can determine the winner.

These cameras turn on the instant the starting pistol fires. They connect to a laser beam at the finish line. When a runner crosses the beam, the cameras capture the moment. They record thousands of frames per second. If the race is close, officials can replay the ending frame by frame to see who won.

Distance events such as the marathon do not use laser beams. Instead, runners wear special tags on their shoes. Mats at the start line pick up the tags' signals. Mats every 5 kilometres (3.1 miles) track the runners' progress. Mats at the finish line records each runner's final time.

Lasers and cameras help ensure medals are correctly awarded in close finishes.

## Keeping cool

When an athlete's muscles burn energy, they create lots of heat. The body needs to cool itself down – but how?

One trick is to send more blood to the skin. The outside air cools the blood before it flows back through the body. Another solution is sweat. Sweat is a liquid made by glands in the skin. It consists of water and small amounts of minerals, including sodium, potassium and calcium. When the sweat **evaporates** into the air, it takes heat with it. Marathon runners may sweat 3.8 litres (1 gallon) of water during a race. They must drink a lot to replace the water they lose.

**evaporate** to change from a liquid into a vapour

British athlete Greg Rutherford leaped to a gold-medal finish in the long jump in the 2012 London Olympics.

# CHAPTER 3

# ONE GIANT *LEAP*

Could you jump the length of two cars? Or leap over a yellow box road sign? An Olympic jumper could!

To make their jaw-dropping leaps, athletes must fight the downward force of gravity. Every object has a **centre of gravity**. This is the point where it would balance if you hung it from a string. When a person is standing still, his or her centre of gravity is close to the navel. The centre of gravity shifts as the body position changes. Olympic jumpers have to control their centres of gravity when they jump. By moving their arms and legs to adjust their centres of gravity, top athletes can jump higher and further in their quests for medal-winning performances.

**centre of gravity** point at which an object's weight is centred

centre
of gravity

## A running jump

Long jumpers and triple jumpers sprint down a 40-metre (131-foot) track to gain speed. Then they leap into a sand pit. Their running speed gives them momentum. Even after their feet leave the ground, this momentum carries them forwards in the air. The faster athletes run, the more momentum they have, and the further they can jump. This is why many athletes do well at both sprinting and jumping events.

Once in the air, a long jumper swings her legs up and forwards. This pulls her centre of gravity forwards. The forward and upward movement of her legs allows her to reach a longer distance. She travels further before touching the sand. The jump is measured to the mark she made in the sand while landing.

# CENTRE OF GRAVITY

American athlete Janay DeLoach Soukup stretches out her legs for landing in the long jump final during the 2012 London Olympics.

## Jumping high

High jumpers must run and throw their bodies over a bar. The bar moves up each round. The last remaining jumper wins. The men's world record is just over 2.44 metres (8 feet). The women's record is 2.08 metres (6 feet, 10 inches).

The athlete has to raise his centre of gravity as high as possible. After a short run, he launches himself into the air. Jumpers once leaped over the bar face down. But in the 1960s, an American athlete named Dick Fosbury had a better idea. He twisted his body while jumping to go over the bar face up. It allowed him to clear higher bars without raising his centre of gravity higher. It also made it less likely that an elbow or knee would bump the bar. Fosbury took home the gold medal at the 1968 Mexico City Olympics. This method is now known as the Fosbury Flop.

Dick Fosbury set a new record at the 1968 Mexico City Olympics using his revolutionary high jump technique.

## THE FOSBURY *FLOP*

High jumpers run towards the bar, then turn to leap over it face up and backwards. This technique is called the Fosbury Flop.

## Acrobatic athletes

The highest jumpers of all are the pole vaulters. Imagine jumping over a giraffe. That's how high these athletes soar! They vault over a bar using a long pole made of fibreglass and carbon fibre. These materials are strong but flexible. They quickly spring back after they bend.

Pole vaulters use two different kinds of energy in their jumps: **kinetic energy** and **potential energy**. Kinetic energy is the energy of motion. Potential energy is stored energy.

An enormous amount of energy is stored in the pole as it bends.

**kinetic energy** energy of motion
**potential energy** stored energy

The pole stores energy briefly, then transfers it back to the athlete as it moves him over the crossbar.

The vaulter sprints down a 40-metre (131-foot) track called a runway. This creates kinetic energy. She slams the pole into a small box. The vaulter's energy transfers to the bending pole as potential energy. As the pole straightens, it changes back into kinetic energy. It pushes the vaulter up and over the bar.

The vaulter drives her feet toward the sky, lifting her centre of gravity as high as possible. At the top of the bar, she is upside down. She swings her feet over the bar and pushes the pole away. If all goes well, she lands on her back on the soft mat below.

Chilean athlete Natalia Ducó hurls the shot in the 2012 London Olympics.

# CHAPTER 4

# THROWING
# COMPETITIONS

People have been throwing stones for thousands of years. The Ancient Greeks held rock-throwing contests. Soldiers in the Middle Ages tossed cannonballs. Today, Olympians hurl lead balls the size of grapefruits. These are called shots. A shot weighs 4 kilograms (8.8 pounds) for women and 7.3 kilograms (16 pounds) for men. It takes great strength and skill to push this heavy weight through the air.

Shot putters must stay inside a circle that is 2.1 metres (7 feet) across. They spin around, making either a half turn or one and a half turns, depending on their chosen technique. During the spin, the athletes exert **centripetal force** to prevent the rotation from carrying the shot away. Then they release the shot. The distance is determined by the speed of rotation, which gives momentum to the ball, and the shot putter's arm muscles, which add power to the motion.

**centripetal force** force that holds an object along a curved path

## Hammer it home

The hammer throwing event involves a ball that is hooked to a cable. This "hammer" weighs the same as a shot. But it goes up to four times further. How can this be?

The secret is the length of the cable. It lets the ball move in a larger circle than the shot does. The ball builds up more speed by the time it is released. The extra speed gives it more momentum and allows it to travel further. When the athlete releases the cable, the hammer travels in an arc from the point of release.

China's Zhang Wenxiu prepares to release in the hammer throw event in the 2012 London Olympics.

## Throwing spears

Javelin throwers heave long, pointed spears down the field. The thrower takes a running start to build momentum. When he stops, the energy travels up through his body and into the javelin. An extra push from his arm muscles makes it fly even further.

Japanese athlete Genki Dean makes a throw in the javelin finals at the 2012 London Olympics.

## Flying saucers

The discus looks a bit like a frisbee, but you wouldn't want to try catching one! This flat saucer is made of wood, rubber or plastic with a metal rim. The men's discus weighs 2 kilograms (4.4 pounds). The women's is smaller and lighter at 1 kilogram (2.2 pounds).

The discus flies straight out from the point where it is released. The flat disk cuts through the air. Its shape helps it stay aloft, like an aeroplane's wing. The air moves faster over the discus than under it. This causes a difference in air pressure that lifts the discus and helps it stay in the air.

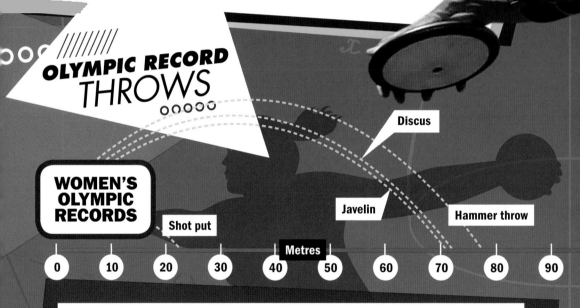

**OLYMPIC RECORD THROWS**

**WOMEN'S OLYMPIC RECORDS**

Discus

Javelin

Hammer throw

Shot put

Metres

0  10  20  30  40  50  60  70  80  90

| Event | Athlete | Year | Mark (m) | Country |
|-------|---------|------|----------|---------|
| Discus | Martina Hellmann | 1988 | 72.30 | East Germany** |
| Hammer throw | Tatyana Lysenko | 2012 | 78.18 | Russia |
| Javelin | Osleidys Menéndez | 2004 | 71.53 | Cuba |
| Shot put | Ilona Slupianek | 1980 | 22.41 | East Germany** |

*The Soviet Union split into several countries in 1991, including Russia.
**Germany split into East and West Germany in 1949. They joined together again to form modern Germany in 1990.

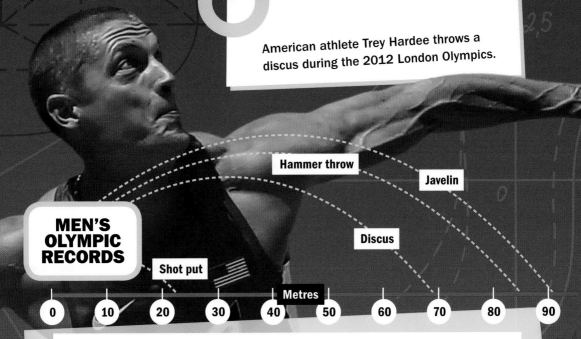

American athlete Trey Hardee throws a discus during the 2012 London Olympics.

**MEN'S OLYMPIC RECORDS**

Hammer throw

Javelin

Discus

Shot put

Metres

0  10  20  30  40  50  60  70  80  90

| Event | Athlete | Year | Mark (m) | Country |
|---|---|---|---|---|
| Discus | Virgilijus Alekna | 2004 | 69.89 | Lithuania |
| Hammer throw | Sergey Litvinov | 1988 | 84.80 | Soviet Union* |
| Javelin | Andreas Thorkildsen | 2008 | 90.57 | Norway |
| Shot put | Ulf Timmermann | 1988 | 22.47 | East Germany** |

## *Always advancing*

Today scientists study what an athlete should eat to perform well. They research the best ways to move and to practice. They keep making better shoes and faster tracks. Athletes learn how to take advantage of the laws of physics to increase their distances and cut their finishing times.

Is there a limit to how fast humans can run, how high they can jump and how far they can throw? No one really knows. But advances in science, technology and talent are sure to keep bringing new Olympic records.

# GLOSSARY

**centre of gravity** point at which an object's weight is centred

**centripetal force** force that holds an object along a curved path

**draft** to run close behind another runner to lessen air resistance

**drag** force that slows an object in motion travelling in air or water

**endurance** ability to remain active for a long time

**evaporate** to change from a liquid into a vapour

**gravity** force that causes objects to move towards Earth's centre

**kinetic energy** energy of motion

**momentum** mass of an object multiplied by its speed

**potential energy** stored energy

# READ MORE

*Children's Book of Sport* (Dorling Kindersley, 2011).

*Track Athletics* (Know Your Sport), Clive Gifford (Franklin Watts, 2012).

*Usain Bolt* (Inspirational Lives), Simon Hart (Wayland, 2012).

# COMPREHENSION QUESTIONS

1. Study the graphs on pages 28–29. Which thrown objects travelled the furthest? Why? How do the factors of gravity and air resistance come into play?

2. The graph on pages 10–11 shows how race times have become faster over the past century. The laws of physics that affect runners, such as air resistance and gravity, have not changed. What factors may have led to these decreased times?

# WEBSITES

BBC: Athletics
*http://www.bbc.com/sport/0/athletics*
Read the latest headlines about athletics.

BBC: How to Get into Athletics
*http://www.bbc.com/sport/0/get-inspired/23143014*
Learn about your options for competing in athletics.

Olympic.org: Athletics
*http://www.olympic.org/athletics*
Explore the rich history of athletics at the Olympics.

# INDEX